George Swan Nottage

The Shakspearian Diary and Almanack

A daily Chronicle of Events, with appropriate Quotations from the Poet's

Works

George Swan Nottage

The Shakspearian Diary and Almanack
A daily Chronicle of Events, with appropriate Quotations from the Poet's Works

ISBN/EAN: 9783337119133

Printed in Europe, USA, Canada, Australia, Japan

Cover: Foto ©ninafisch / pixelio.de

More available books at **www.hansebooks.com**

THE CAST

FROM

THE FACE OF SHAKSPEARE

After DEATH, 1616.

Extracts from " Friswell's Life Portraits of William Shakspeare."

The History is as follows :—

A German nobleman had an ancestor who was attached to one of the ambassadors accredited to the Court of King James I. This gentleman was, like many of his countrymen at a later period, a great admirer of the genius of Shakspeare, and as a memorial of him, bought the Cast, in all probability from the sculptor of his tomb, Gerard Johnson ; had it carefully preserved, and took it with him to his own country. There it was shown in his castle, and looked upon with much awe by his friends and neighbours.* The nobleman who brought it home employed a pupil of Vandyke to paint the miniature which accompanied it. The mask and miniature remained in the family, and descended from father to son for many generations, until they came into the possession of the last of the family, a dignitary of the Church in Cologne.† Dr. Becker (the brother to the Secretary of the late Prince Consort) purchased the Cast and also the miniature, and about twelve years since, lodged them in the private possession of Professor Owen, but subsequently the brother of Dr. Becker took it back to Germany. It is believed that Dr. Becker perished in the disastrous South Australian expedition.

All the original legal documents connected with this precious Relic were likewise in the possession of Professor Owen. Amongst them was a letter from Professor Muller, stating that the Kessalsdadt family kept up a lively commerce in works of art with London for nearly 300 years, and that they had a 'arge collection of the Portraits of Gustavus Adolphus, Henry IV., Luther, Melancthon, &c., &c., and that among the *savans* who visited the collection, not the least doubt existed as to the authenticity of the Shakspeare Relic.

It has been admirably and artistically posed and copied by the Stereoscopic Company, and the mask of the face of the dead Poet, reposing on a rich velvet, and wearing the drawn and refined expression of Death, as well as its calm repose, is a very striking one.　　　　　　HAIN FRISWELL.

The late Chief Baron Pollock, after considering the whole of the historical evidence laid before him by Professor Owen, declared that if called upon to pronounce a judicial decision, it would be that it was none other than the Cast from the Head and Face of Shakspeare.

* Fanny Kemble was so much impressed with its vivid truthfulness, that on seeing it she burst into tears.
† The back of the Cast bears the inscription—A.D. 1616—the year Shakspeare died.

THE

Shakspeare, William

SHAKSPEARIAN DIARY

AND

Almanack.

A DAILY CHRONICLE OF EVENTS,

WITH

APPROPRIATE QUOTATIONS

FROM THE POET'S WORKS.

Prefatory Note.

THAT works, written from two hundred and fifty to three hundred years since, should furnish an apt and appropriate quotation against each daily event recorded in the following pages, is another proof of the marvellous, and almost miraculous, power and versatility of Shakspeare's genius,* and will impress the mind, perhaps, more forcibly than many works of a more elaborate and ambitious character, that our great master-spirit " was not for an age, but

"FOR ALL TIME."

This little work is another tribute laid humbly upon his shrine.

---

* It may be mentioned incidentally, and as a fact not generally known, that the late Lord Palmerston was of opinion—and this he expressed to the writer—that Shakspeare did *not* write the plays which pass as his productions, but that his name was merely used to introduce them to the world. The main point or principle in his argument was, that as these works are admitted by all to be the greatest works of any age or country, was it in any degree probable that they should be the productions of an actor, actively engaged in his profession, born in a provincial town, and with comparatively no education? On the other hand, there was *one* man living at the time these works were produced, whose great intellect, extended knowledge, and profound philosophy were equal to their production, and, therefore, BACON, and not Shakspeare, wrote "Shakspeare." It was easy to answer these arguments, but not easy to convince the veteran statesman that the facts were all against him. It is singular that the practical mind of Lord Palmerston should have harboured, and so stoutly defended, such an opinion.

NOTE.

The ruled lines are intended for the admirers of the great poet to make other quotations appropriate to the events which their memories may recall, and which may possibly be more striking than the one selected by the compiler. Thus, for the event on the 15th April (the Boat-Race), another very apt quotation might strike the reader in the play of Henry VI., which he would do well to record :—

"*O cheerful colours! see where OXFORD comes!*"

"No day without a deed to crown it."

Hen. VIII. v. 4.

JANUARY.

1	F	THE OVEREND GURNEY PROSECUTION *com.* 1869. *"There's theft in 'limited' professions"* . .	A. SC. *T. of A.* iv. 3.
2	S	GEN. WOLFE *b.* 1727. *"Undaunted spirit in a dying breast"* . .	1 *H. VI.* iii. 2.
3	S	**Second after Christmas.** *"We are in God's hand, brother"* . .	*Hen. V.* iii. 6.
4	M	ARREST OF THE FIVE MEMBERS, 1641–2, BY CHARLES I. *"This is the way to lay the city flat;* *To bring the roof to the foundation;* *And bury all, which yet distinctly ranges,* *In heaps and piles of ruin"*	*Corio.* iii. 1.
5	T	CATHERINE DE MEDICIS *d.* 1589. *"Haughty spirit, winged with desire"* .	3 *Hen. VI.* i. 1.
6	W	BEN. FRANKLIN *b.* 1706. *"And when the cross blue lightning seemed to open* *The breast of Heaven, he did present himself* *Even in the aim and very flash of it"* . .	*Jul. C.* i. 3.
7	Th	CHAS. DICKENS *b.* 1812. *"More, more, I pr'ythee, more"*	*A.Y.L.I.* ii. 5.
8	F	GALILEO *d.* 1642. *"O, learned indeed were that astronomer"* .	*Cym.* iii. 2.
9	S	THE DAVY LAMP FIRST USED, 1816. *"'Tis our safety, and we must embrace the gentle offer"*	*K. John* iv. 3.
10	S	**First after Epiphany.** *"Open thy gate of mercy, gracious God"*	3 *H. VI.* i. 4.
11	M	WRECK OF THE "LONDON," 1866. *"The sailors sought for safety by our boat,* *And left the ship"*	*C. of E.* i. 1.
12	T	SIR ROBERT HARRY INGLIS *b.* 1786. *"A loyal, just, and upright gentleman"* . .	*Rich. II.* i. 3.
13	W	CHARLES JAMES FOX *b.* 1748 *"Remember, I have done thee worthy service"*	*Tempest* i. 2.
14	Th	CAPT. MAURY *b.* 1806. *"The current that with gentle murmur glides,* *Thou know'st"*	*T.G. of V.* ii. 7.
15	F	DR. PARR *b.* 1747. *"I'll talk a word with this same learned Theban"*	*K. Lear* iii. 4.

JANUARY.

16	S	BATTLE OF CORUNNA, 1809.	A. SC.
		" Doubtfully it stood " . . .	*Mac.* i. 2.
17	☽	Second Sunday after Epiphany.	
		" Words without thoughts never to Heaven go "	*Ham.* iii. 2.
18	M	CHARLES KEAN *b.* 1811.	
		" Accounted a good actor " .	*Ham.* iii. 2.
19	T	BESSEMER *b.* 1813.	
		" A man of steel " . . .	*A. & C.* iv. 2.
20	W	FIRST PARLIAMENT MET 1265.	
		" God speed the Parliament " . .	*1 H. IV.* iii. 2.
21	Th	"DAILY NEWS" ESTABLISHED, 1846.	
		" Honest and fair "	*Ham.* iii. 1.
22	F	DEATH OF THE YOUNG PRINCE OF BELGIUM, 1869.	
		" Grief fills the room up of my absent child,	
		Lies in his bed, walks up and down with me,	
		Puts on his pretty looks, repeats his words,	
		Remembers me of all his gracious parts." .	*K. John* iii. 4.
23	S	TREATY OF COMMERCE SIGNED 1860.	
		" France friend with England " . . .	*K. John* iii. 1.
24	☽	Septuagesima.	
		" In the great hand of God I stand " . .	*Mac.* ii. 3.
25	M	ROB. BURNS *b.* 1759.	
		" The first that ever Scotland	
		In such an honour named " .	*Mac.* v. 7.
26	T	DR. JENNER *d.* 1823.	
		" Dost thou forget	
		From what a torment I did free thee ? " .	*Temp.* i. 2.
27	W	RD. BURTON *b.* 1639.	
		" A most rare boy of melancholy " . .	*Cym.* iv. 2.
28	Th	ABDICATION OF JAMES II. VOTED BY HOUSE OF COMMONS, 1688.	
		" The people's enemy is gone "	*Corio.* iii. 3.
29	F	ROEBUCK ENTERED PARLIAMENT, 1833.	
		" He hath a heart as sound as a bell, and his	
		tongue is the clapper ;	
		For what his heart thinks his tongue speaks "	*M. Ado* iii. 2.
30	S	CHARLES I. EXECUTED, 1649.	
		" Uneasy lies the head that wears a crown " .	*2 H. IV.* iii. 1.
31	☽	Sexagesima.	
		" Blessed are the peace-makers " .	*2 H. VI.* ii. 1.

FEBRUARY.

			A. SC.
1	M	JOHN KEMBLE *b*. 1757. "*Murder thy breath in middle of a word,* *And then again begin, and stop again* *As if thou wert distraught, and mad with terror*"	*Ric. III*. iii. 5.
2	T	BEAU NASH *d*. 1761. "*There can be no kernel in this light nut: the* *soul of this man is his clothes*" . .	*All's Well* ii. 5.
3	W	JENNY LIND *b*. 1820. "*Sings as sweetly as a nightingale*" .	*Tam. Sh*. ii. 1.
4	Th	BLAIR *d*. 1746. "*My joy is—death;* *Death at whose name I oft have been afeard*".	*2 Hen. VI*. ii. 4.
5	F	SIR ROB. PEEL *b*. 1788. "*I have bought golden opinions from all sorts* *of people*"	*Mac*. i. 7.
6	S	SWINBURNE *b*. 1843. "*Give me an ounce of civet, good apothecary, to* *sweeten my imagination*" . . .	*K. Lear* iv. 6.
7	☰	Quinquagesima. "*There's a divinity that shapes our ends,* *Rough-hew them how we will*"	*Ham*. v. 2.
8	M	RUSKIN *b*. 1819. "*Of imagination all compact*" .	*M. N. D*. v. 1.
9	T	"*A pancake for Shrove Tuesday*" . . .	*All's Well* ii. 2.
10	W	MARRIAGE OF Q. VICTORIA & PRINCE ALBERT, 1840. "*Whose love was of that dignity* *That it went hand-in-hand, even with the vow* *He made to her in marriage*" . . .	*Ham*. i. 5.
11	Th	QUEEN MARY *b*. 1516. "*The bloody-minded Queen*" . . .	*3 Hen. VI*. ii. 6.
12	F	SIR ASTLEY COOPER *d*. 1841. "*By medicine life may be prolonged, yet death* *Will seize the doctor too*"	*Cym*. v. 5.
13	S	CHOLERA FIRST APPEARED IN LONDON, 1832. "*We cannot hold mortality's strong hand*" .	*K. John* iv. 2.
14	☰	First Sunday in Lent. "*O upright, true, and just-disposing God* *How do I thank thee.*" .	*Ric. III*. iv. 4.

FEBRUARY.

15	M	CAPT. COOK KILLED, 1779.	
		"*Murdered by savage islanders*"	*2 Hen. VI.* iv. 1.
16	T	MELANCTHON *b.* 1497.	
		"*A gentle, noble temper,*	
		A soul as even as a calm"	*H. VIII.* iii. 1.
17	W	PEPYS *b.* 1632-3.	
		"*My book, wherein my soul recorded*	
		The history of all her secret thoughts"	*K. Lear* iv. 6.
18	Th	GEORGE PEABODY *b.* 1795.	
		"*A most incomparable man*"	*T. of A.* i. 1.
		"*The heart of generosity*"	*Corio.* i. 1.
19	F	SIR RODERICK MURCHISON *b.* 1792.	
		"*Sermons in stones*"	*A.Y.L.I.* ii. 1.
20	S	JOSEPH HUME *d.* 1855.	
		"*What is the figure? What is the figure?*"	*L. L. L.* v. 1.
21	℺	Second Sunday in Lent.	
		"*The will of Heaven be done*"	*H. VIII.* i. 1.
22	M	WASHINGTON *b.* 1732.	
		"*I led my country's strength successfully*"	*Tit. And.* i. 2.
23	T	SYDNEY SMITH *d.* 1845.	
		"*Your flashes of merriment that were wont to*	
		set the table in a roar"	*Ham.* v. 1.
24	W	KEATS *d.* 1821.	
		"*We are such stuff*	
		As dreams are made of, and our little life	
		Is rounded with a sleep"	*Tempest* iv. 1.
25	Th	SIR CHRISTOPHER WREN *d.* 1723.	
		"*This grave shall have a living monument*"	*Ham.* v. 1.
26	F	DR. KITCHENER *d.* 1827.	
		"*But his neat cookery! He cut our roots in*	
		character;	
		And sauc'd our broths"	*Cym.* iv. 2.
27	S	LONGFELLOW *b.* 1807.	
		"*That happy verse*	
		Which aptly sings the good"	*T. of A.* i. 1.
28	℺	Third Sunday in Lent.	
		"*Go to your bosom;*	
		Knock there; and ask your heart, what it doth	
		know"	*M. for M.* ii. 2.

MARCH.

			A. SC.
1	M	ST. DAVID. *"No scorn to wear the leek Upon Saint Tavy's Day"*	*Hen. V.* iv. 7.
2	T	JOHN WESLEY *d.* 1791. *"And, to add greater honours to his age Than man could give, he died, fearing God"* .	*H.VIII.* iv. 2.
3	W	GEORGE HERBERT *d.* 1633. *"Holy and heavenly thoughts"* . . .	*H.VIII.* v. 4.
4	Th	MACREADY *b.* 1793. RETIRED FEB. 26, 1851. *"A well-graced actor leaves the stage"* . .	*Rich. II.* v. 2.
5	F	LAYARD *b.* 1817. *"My ancient skill beguiles me"* . .	*M.forM.* iv. 2.
6	S	DEATH OF CHARLES II. *"Nothing extenuate, Nor set down aught in malice"* .	*Oth.* v. 2.
7	S	Fourth Sunday in Lent. *"All that live must die; Passing through Nature to Eternity"* .	*Ham.* i. 2.
8	M	WILLIAM COBBETT *b.* 1762. *"And as you know me all, a plain, blunt man"*	*Jul. C.* iii. 2.
9	T	CARD. MAZARINE *d.* 1661. *"More like a soldier than a man o' the Church"*	*2 H. VI.* i. 1.
10	W	PRINCE OF WALES MARRIED, 1863. *"Smile, Heaven, upon this fair conjunction"* .	*Ric. III.* v. 4.
11	Th	DR. LIVINGSTONE *b.* 1817. *"I have watched, and travelled hard"* . .	*K. Lear* ii. 2.
12	F	CHELSEA HOSPITAL FOUNDED, 1682. *"Look, sir;—my wounds:— I got them in my country's service"* .	*Corio.* ii. 3.
13	S	DR. PRIESTLEY *b.* 1733. *"Was he not held a learned man?"* .	*H. VIII.* ii. 2.
14	S	Fifth Sunday in Lent. *"Charity itself fulfils the law"*	*L. L. L.* iv. 3.
15	M	ADMIRAL BYNG SHOT, 1757. *"A guiltless death I die"*	*Oth.* v. 2.
16	T	HEIR TO NAPOLEON III. *b.* 1856. *"The Heavens have blessed you with a goodly son To be your comforter"*	*Ric. III.* i. 3.

MARCH.

17	W	ST. PATRICK'S DAY. " *Now for our Irish wars*"	A. SC. *Rich. II.* ii. 1.
18	Th	SIR ROB. WALPOLE *d.* 1745. " *Much condemned to have an itching palm,* *To sell and mart your offices for gold*" . .	*Jul. C.* iv. 3.
19	F	HORNE TOOKE *d.* 1812. " *Yield me roots*"	*T. of A.* iv. 3.
20	S	SIR ISAAC NEWTON *d.* 1727. " *Is as the very centre of the earth,* *Drawing all things to it*" * . . .	*T. & C.* iv. 2.
21	S	Palm Sunday. " *God bless thee; and put meekness in thy breast,* *Love, charity, obedience, and true duty*" .	*Ric. III.* ii. 2.
22	M	ROSA BONHEUR *b.* 1822. " *Look, when a painter would surpass the life,* *In limning out a well-proportioned steed*" .	*V. and Adonis.*
23	T	ENGLAND LAID UNDER INTERDICT, 1208. " *No Italian priest shall tithe or toll in our* *dominions*"	*K. John* iii. 1.
24	W	QUEEN ELIZABETH *d.* 1603. " *Great Albion's Queen*"	3 *H. VI.* iii. 3.
25	Th	MURAT *b.* 1771. " *Fortune, oh!* *She is corrupted, changed, and won from thee*"	*K. John* iii. 1.
26	F	GOOD FRIDAY. " *Christ's dear blood shed for our grievous sins*"	*Ric. III.* i. 4.
27	S	DR. RUSSELL *b.* 1821. " *'List his discourse of war, and you shall hear* *A fearful battle render'd you in music*" . .	*Hen. V.* i. 1.
28	S	Easter Sunday. " *All the souls that were, were forfeit once:* *And He, that might th' vantage best have took,* *Found out the remedy*"	*M. for M.* ii. 2.
29	M	LORD DERBY *b.* 1799. " *Hath all the good gifts of nature*" . .	*Twel. N.* i. 3.
30	T	DR. HUNTER *d.* 1783. " *He was famous, sir, in his profession, and* *it was his great right to be so*" . .	*All's W.* i. 1.
31	W	HAYDN *b.* 1732. " *Sweet airs that give delight*"	*Temp.* iii. 2.

* Is not Sir J. Newton's great discovery here anticipated.

APRIL.

			A. SC.
1	Th	ALL FOOLS' DAY.	
		" It is a custom	
		More honoured in the breach than the observance"	*Ham.* i. 4.
2	F	BATTLE OF COPENHAGEN, 1802.	
		" Our indiscretion sometimes serves us well" .	*Ham.* v. 2.
3	S	PROF. WILSON (CHRISTOPHER NORTH) *d.* 1854.	
		" Bright and jovial"	*Mac.* iii. 2.
4	☉	First Sunday after Easter.	
		" The means that Heaven yields must be embraced	
		And not neglected"	*Rich. II.* iii. 2.
5	M	STOW *d.* 1605.	
		" An honest chronicler"	*H. VIII.* iv. 2.
6	T	DR. BUSBY *d.* 1695.	
		" Take hence this Jack, and whip him" . .	*A. & C.* iii. 11.
7	W	WORDSWORTH *b.* 1770.	
		" Exempt from public haunts,	
		Finds tongues in trees, books in running brooks,	
		Sermons in stones, and good in everything" .	*A.Y.L.I.* ii. 1.
8	Th	HUMBOLDT *d.* 1835.	
		" He was skilful enough to have lived still if	
		knowledge could be set up against mortality"	*All's Well* i. 1.
9	F	PATTI *b.* 1843.	
		" She sings like one immortal" . . .	*Peric.* iii. 5.
10	S	GROTIUS *b.* 1583.	
		" Of singular integrity and learning" . .	*H. VIII.* ii. 4.
11	☉	Second Sunday after Easter.	
		" Let never day nor night unhallowed pass	
		But still remember what the Lord hath done"	*2 Hen. VI.* ii. 1.
12	M	HENRY CLAY *b.* 1777.	
		" A good member of the Commonwealth" . .	*L.L.L.* iv. 2.
13	T	HANDEL *d.* 1759.	
		" A solemn air, the best comforter	
		To an unsettled fancy"	*Tempest* v. 1.
14	W	PRESIDENT LINCOLN SHOT, 1865.	
		" Premeditated and contrived murder " . .	*Hen. V.* iv. 5.
15	Th	UNIVERSITY BOAT RACE INSTITUTED, 1829.	
		" 'Tis deeds must win the prize" . . .	*Tam. Sh.* ii. 1.

APRIL.

			A. SC.
16	F	BATTLE OF CULLODEN, 1746.	
		"*The common course of all treasons*" . .	*All's Well* iv. 3.
17	S	MISS BURDETT COUTTS *b.* 1814.	
		"*Most bounteous lady*"	*Tempest* iv. 1.
18	☉	Third Sunday after Easter.	
		" *O Lord that lend'st me life,*	
		Lend me a heart replete with thankfulness" .	2 *Hen. VI.* i. 1.
19	M	JUDGE JEFFRIES *d.* 1689.	
		"*Thou hast a cruel nature and a bloody*" . .	*H. VIII.* v. 2.
20	T	NAPOLEON III. *b.* 1808.	
		"*Here comes the Emperor :*	
·		*Is't not strange ?*"	*A. & C.* iii. 7.
21	W	THE "STANDARD" ESTABLISHED, 1827.	
		"*By the excellent Constitution*" . .	*Tw. N.* i. 3.
22	Th	FROUDE *b.* 1818.	
		"*Stand forth : and with a bold spirit relate what you*	
		Most like a careful subject have collected" .	*H. VIII.* i. 1.
23	F	ST. GEORGE'S DAY. Shakspeare *b.* 1564 ; *d.*	
		April 23, 1616.	
		"*Every god did seem to set his seal*	
		To give the world assurance of a man" . .	*Ham.* iii. 4.
		"*How noble in reason ! How infinite in*	
		faculties ! * *	
		In action how like an angel ! In apprehen-	
		sion how like a god !" . . .	*Ham.* ii. 2.
24	S	TRIAL OF WARREN HASTINGS CONCLUDED, 1795.	
		"*It would be too tedious to repeat*" . .	*Peric.* v. 1.
25	☉	Fourth Sunday after Easter.	
		" *God's goodness hath been great to thee*"	2 *Hen. VI.* ii. 1.
26	M	MRS. HEMANS *d.* 1835.	
		"*Words sweetly placed*" . .	1 *Hen. VI.* v. 3.
27	T	PRESIDENT GRANT *b.* 1822.	
		"*He's a tried and valiant soldier*" . .	*Jul. C.* iv. 1.
28	W	LORD SHAFTESBURY *b.* 1801.	
		"*He hath a tear for pity, and a hand*	
		Open as day for melting charity" . . .	2 *H. IV.* iv. 4.
29	Th	DUCHESS OF GLOUCESTER *d.* 1857. (Last of the family of George III.)	
		"*The last hour of my long weary life has come*	
		upon me"	*H. VIII.* ii. 1.
30	F	RT. HON. J. E. DENISON ELECTED SPEAKER, 1857.	
		"*The speaker in his Parliament*" . .	2 *H. IV.* iv. 2.

MAY.

			A. SC.
1	S	WELLINGTON *b.* 1769. *" The noble nature,* *Whom passion could not shake, whose solid virtue* *The shot of accident, nor dart of chance* *Could neither graze nor pierce"*	*Oth.* iv. 1.
2	S	Rogation Sunday. *" O God! defend my soul!"* .	*Rich. II.* i. 1.
3	M	THOS. HOOD *d.* 1845. *" A merrier man,* *Within the limits of becoming mirth,* *I never spent an hour's talk withal"* .	*L. L. L.* ii. 1.
4	T	EMPRESS EUGENIE *b.* MAY, 1826. *" Of all sorts enchantingly beloved"* . .	*A.Y.L.I.* i. 1.
5	W	NAPOLEON *d.* 1821. *" Ambition's debt is paid"*	*Jul. C.* iii. 1.
6	Th	HALLAM *b.* 1777. *" I wish no other herald,* *No other speaker of my living actions,* *To keep mine honour from corruption,* *But such an honest chronicler"* . . .	*H.VIII.* iv. 2.
7	F	WILKES RELEASED FROM THE TOWER, 1763. *" The Commons made* *A shower, and thunder, with their caps and shouts"*	*Corio.* ii. 1.
8	S	MASSACRE OF GLENCOE, 1691. *" Most grievous, guilty murder"* . .	*Ric. III.* i. 4.
9	S	First Sunday after Ascension. *" Heaven, set ope thy everlasting gates* *To entertain my vows of thanks and praise"* .	*2 H. VI.* iv. 9.
10	M	LOUIS XV. *d.* 1774. *" All's done!—here breathless lies the King"* .	*1 H. IV.* v. 3.
11	T	PANIC IN THE CITY, 1866. *" Fellows ran about the streets* *Crying, Confusion!"*	*Corio.* iv. 6.
12	W	EARL STRAFFORD BEHEADED, 1641. *" Oh! how wretched* *Is that poor man that hangs on princes' favours"*	*H.VIII.* iii. 2.
13	Th	CUVIER *d.* 1832. *" Thou, Nature, art my goddess; to thy law* *My services are bound"*	*K. Lear* i. 2.
14	F	GRATTAN *d.* 1820. *" The power of speech* *To stir men's blood"*	*Jul. C.* ii. 2.
15	S	FLORENCE NIGHTINGALE *b.* 1820. *" Lowliness, devotion, patience, courage"* . .	*Mac.* iv. 3.

MAY.

16	S	**Whit Sunday.**	A. SC.
		"Heavenly power, guide us" .	*Temp.* v. 1.
17	M	ROB. BROWNING *b.* 1812.	
		"There's more in me than thou understandst" .	*T. & C.* iv. 5.
18	T	BONAPARTE MADE EMPEROR, 1804.	
		"He doth bestride the narrow world Like a colossus"	*Jul. C.* i. 2.
19	W	THACKERAY *b.* 1811.	
		"Sharp and sententious; pleasant, without scurrility; Witty, without affection; audacious, without impudency; Learned, without opinion; and strange, without heresy"	*L. L. L.* v. 1.
20	Th	NINON DE L'ENCLOS *d.* 1705.	
		"Beauty doth vanish age, as if new born, And gives the crutch the cradle's infancy" .	*L. L. L.* iv. 3.
21	F	MARIA EDGEWORTH *d.* 1849.	
		"Revolve what tales I have told you" .	*Cym.* iii. 3.
22	S	GRISI *b.* 1812.	
		"Thou sing'st sweet music" . .	*Ric. III.* iv. 2.
23	S	**Trinity Sunday.**	
		"Now God be praised, that to believing souls Gives light in darkness, comfort in despair	*2 H. VI.* ii. 1.
24	M	QUEEN VICTORIA *b.* 1819.	
		"Madam, all joy befall your grace!" .	*Cym.* iii. 5.
25	T	PRINCESS HELENA *b.* 1846.	
		"God bless thee, lady" . .	*Twel. N.* i. 5.
26	W	WILKIE COLLINS *b.* 1824.	
		"I could a tale unfold, whose lightest word Would harrow up thy soul" . . .	*Ham.* i. 5.
27	Th	THOMAS MOORE *b.* 1779.	
		"A bard of Ireland" . .	*Ric. III.* iv. 2.
28	F	W. PITT *b.* 1759.	
		"How youngly he began to serve his country; How long continued!"	*Corio.* ii. 3.
29	S	THE ENTRY OF CHARLES II. INTO THE CITY.	
		"Now London doth pour out her citizens, With the plebeians swarming at their heels" .	*Hen. V.* v. ch.
30	S	**First Sunday after Trinity.**	
		"Confess yourself to Heaven, Repent what's past" . .	*Ham.* iii. 3.
31	M	GRIMALDI *d.* 1837.	
		"I had rather have a fool to make me merry than experience to make me sad" . .	*A. Y. L. I.* iv. 1.

JUNE.

1	T	**LORD HOWE'S VICTORY, 1794.** "*The harder matched, the greater victory*"	A. SC. 3 *Hen. VI*. v. 1.
2	W	**SIR CRESSWELL CRESSWELL** *b.* 1794. "*He will divorce you*"	*Oth.* i. 2.
3	Th	**COBDEN** *b.* 1804. "*When we stood up about the* CORN"	*Corio.* ii. 3.
4	F	**LORD ELDON** *b.* 1751. "*Doubtful whether what I see be true*"	*M. of V.* iii. 2.
5	S	**DR. SACHEVERELL** *d.* 1724. "*That villainous abominable misleader*"	1 *Hen. IV*. ii. 4.
6	☩	𝔖𝔢𝔠𝔬𝔫𝔡 𝔖𝔲𝔫𝔡𝔞𝔶 𝔞𝔣𝔱𝔢𝔯 𝔗𝔯𝔦𝔫𝔦𝔱𝔶. "*O God! forgive my sins!*"	3 *Hen. VI.* v. 6.
7	M	**REFORM BILL PASSED, 1832.** "*Liberty, freedom, and enfranchisement*"	*Jul. C.* iii. 1.
8	T	**SIR JOSEPH PAXTON** *d.* 1865. "*The world's best garden he achieved*"	*H. V.* ii. chorus
9	W	**G. P. BIDDER** *b.* 1800. "*A great arithmetician*"	*Oth.* i. 1.
10	Th	**STEELE** *b.* 1671. "*The web of our life is of a mingled yarn, good and ill together*"	*All's Well* iv. 3.
11	F	**SIR JOHN FRANKLIN** *d.* 1847. "*Entombed upon the very hem o' the sea*"	*T. of A.* v. 5.
12	S	**WHEATSTONE'S TELEGRAPH NEEDLE PATENTED,** 1837. "*The tidings come * * * * * And fly like thought, from them to me again*"	*K. John* iv. 2.
13	☩	𝔗𝔥𝔦𝔯𝔡 𝔖𝔲𝔫𝔡𝔞𝔶 𝔞𝔣𝔱𝔢𝔯 𝔗𝔯𝔦𝔫𝔦𝔱𝔶. "*God's benison go with you*"	*Mac.* ii. 4.
14	M	**FIRST CRUSADE LEFT ENGLAND, 1091.** "*As far as the sepulchre of Christ, Whose soldier now, under whose blessed cross We are impressèd, and engaged to fight*"	1 *Hen. IV.* i. 1.
15	T	**MRS. BEECHER STOWE** *b.* 1814. "*By Heaven, thy love is black as ebony*"	*L. L. L.* iv. 3.

.

JUNE.

			A. SC.
16	W	MARLBOROUGH *d.* 1722. "*Brave captain, and victorious lord*" . .	1 *H. VI.* iii. 4.
17	Th	ACQUITTAL OF THE SEVEN BISHOPS, 1688. "*Rejoice now at this happy news*" . . .	2 *H. IV.* iv. 4.
18	F	BATTLE OF WATERLOO. "*O God! Thy arm was here!* *And not to us but to Thy arm alone* *Ascribe we all*"	*Hen. V.* iv. 8.
19	S	C. H. SPURGEON *b.* 1834. "*Free speech and fearless*" . . .	*Rich. II.* i. 1.
20	♒	ffourth Sunday after Trinity. "*There is a special providence in the fall of a* *sparrow*" .	*Ham.* v. 2.
21	M	ACCESSION OF Q. VICTORIA, JUNE 20, 1837. "*God and His angels guard your sacred throne,* *And make you long become it*" . . .	*Hen. V.* i. 2.
22	T	IMPOSITION OF INCOME TAX, 1842. "*Bull doth bear the yoke*" . .	*M. Ado* i. 1.
23	W	GORDON CUMMING *b.* 1814. "*Talks as familiarly of roaring lions* *As maids of thirteen do of puppy dogs*" .	*K. John* ii. 2.
24	Th	JOHN HAMPDEN *d.* 1643. "*I'll yield myself to prison willingly,* *Or unto death, to do my country good*" .	2 *H. VI.* iv. 9.
25	F	BATTLE OF BANNOCKBURN, 1314. "*What can go well, when we have run so ill?* *Are we not beaten?*"	*K. John* iii. 4.
26	S	DR. DODD EXECUTED, 1777. "*It is a good divine that follows his own in-* *structions*"	*Mer. of V.* i. 2.
27	♒	ffifth Sunday after Trinity. "*All within the will of God*" .	*Hen. V.* i. 2.
28	M	CORONATION DAY, 1838. "*May honourable peace attend thy throne*" .	2 *H. VI.* ii. 3.
29	T	SIR RICHARD MAYNE *b.* 1796. "*Trusted with a muzzle*" . . .	*M. Ado* i. 3.
30	W	HEPWORTH DIXON *b.* 1821. "*I must needs to the Tower*" . . .	*Mer. of V.* i. 2.

JULY.

1	Th	PRINCESS ALICE MARRIED TO PRINCE LOUIS OF HESSE, 1862. *"God, the best maker of all marriages, Combine your hearts in one"* . . .	A. SC. *Hen. V.* v. 2.
2	F	DR. HAHNEMANN *d.* 1843. *"One fire burns out another's burning Take thou some new infection to the eye, And the rank poison of the old will die"* .	*R. & J.* i. 2.
3	S	*"The dog days now reign"* .	*H. VIII.* v. 3.
4	S	Sixth Sunday after Trinity. *"To Thee do I commend my watchful soul Ere I let fall the windows of mine eyes: Sleeping and waking, O defend me still"*	*Ric. III.* v. 3.
5	M	BARNUM *b.* 1810. *"My revenue is the silly cheat"* . .	*Win. T.* iv. 2.
6	T	SIR THOMAS MORE EXECUTED, 1535. *"Be just, and fear not"*	*H. VIII.* iii. 2.
7	W	SHERIDAN *d.* 1816. *"The genius and the mortal"* . . .	*Jul. C.* ii. 1.
8	Th	SIR EDWARD PARRY *d.* 1855. *"A wild dedication of yourselves To unpathed waters, undreamed shores"* . .	*Win. T.* iv. 3.
9	F	ED. BURKE *d.* 1797. *"The gentleman is learned, and a most rare speaker"*	*H. VIII.* i. 2.
10	S	JOHN CALVIN *b.* 1509. *"Of a holy, cold, and still conversation"* . .	*A. & C.* ii. 6.
11	S	Seventh Sunday after Trinity. *"There is no vice so simple, but assumes Some mark of virtue on his outward parts"* .	*M. of V.* iii. 2.
12	M	TITUS OATES *d.* 1704. *"How this world is given to lying!"* .	1 *H. IV.* v. 4.
13	T	DR. MCLEOD *b.* 1812. *"Whate'er you think, 'Good Words,' I think, are best"*	*K. John* iv. 3.
14	W	BASTILLE DESTROYED. 1789. *"Where sighs and groans, and shrieks that rend the air Are made, not marked"*	*Mac.* iv. 3.
15	Th	DUKE OF MONMOUTH BEHEADED, 1685. *"Rash and most unfortunate man"* . .	*Oth.* v. 2.
16	F	SIR JOSHUA REYNOLDS *b.* 1723. *"I'll say of it It tutors nature; artificial strife Lives in these touches, livelier than life"* .	*T. of A.* i. 1.

JULY.

17	S	MARCHIONESS DE BRINVILLIERS EXECUTED, 1676.

       " She did confess she had
         For you a mortal mineral; which, being took,
         Should by the minute feed on life, and, lingering,   A. SC.
         By inches waste you" . . . . . *Cym.* v. 5.

18	S	Eighth Sunday after Trinity.

       " 'Tis mad idolatry
    To make the service greater than the god" . *T. & C.* ii. 2.

19	M	PROFESSOR PLAYFAIR *d.* 1819.

       " I will find
    Where truth is hid, though it were hid indeed
    Within the centre" . . . . *Ham.* iv. 2.

20	T	PROFESSOR OWEN *b.* 1804.

    " Bones bear witness" . . . . . *Win. T.* iv. 4.

21	W	LORD STANLEY *b.* 1826.

    " You showed your judgment" . . . . 3 *H. VI.* iv. 1.

22	Th	WINDOW TAX REPEALED, 1851.

    " If Cæsar can hide the sun from us, or put the
       moon in his pocket, we'll pay him tribute
       for light; else, sir, no more tribute" . *Cym.* iii. 1.

23	F	HYDE PARK DEMONSTRATION, 1866.

    " Have patience, good people" . . . . *A.Y.L.I.* iii. 2.

24	S	CURRAN *b.* 1750.

        " When he speaks
    The air, a chartered libertine, is still,
    And the mute wonder worketh in men's ears,
    To steal his sweet and honeyed sentences" . *Hen. V.* i. 1.

25	S	Ninth Sunday after Trinity.

    " God shall be my hope" . . *2 H. VI.* ii. 3.

26	M	COLERIDGE *d.* 1834.

    " Elegance, facility, and golden cadence o' poesy" . *L. L. L.* iv. 2.

27	T	SPANISH ARMADA DESTROYED, 1588.

    " Clap on more sails; pursue! up with your
       lights!
    Give fire! she is my prize, or ocean whelm
       them all" . . . . . *M. for M.* ii. 2.

28	W	JOHN WALTER *d.* 1847.

    " I witness to the Times" . . . *W. T.* iv. chorus

29	Th	GEORGE GÖSCHEN *b.* 1831.

    " His years but young, but his experience old;
    His head unmellowed, but his judgment ripe" . 2 *G. of V.* ii. 4.

30	F	JEWS' EMANCIPATION ACT (1858)

    " Passed the nobles and the Commons" . . *Cor.* iii. 1.

31	S	SAVAGE *d.* IN PRISON, 1743.

    " Misery acquaints a man with strange bed-fellows" *Tempest.* ii. 2.

AUGUST.

1	☲	**Tenth Sunday after Trinity.** *"Heaven grant us its peace"*	A. SC. *M. for M.* i. 2.
2	M	**LORD HERBERT OF LEA** *d.* 1861. *"I feel within me* *A peace above all earthly dignities—* *A still and quiet conscience"*	*H. VIII.* iii. 2.
3	T	**SIR RICHARD ARKWRIGHT** *d.* 1792. *" My ingenious instrument"* . . .	*Cym.* iv. 2.
4	W	**LORD ELCHO** *b.* 1818. *" We swear a voluntary zeal"*	*K. John* v. 2.
5	Th	**ATLANTIC TELEGRAPH FIRST COMPLETED,** 1858. *" I'll put a girdle round about the earth"* . .	*M.N.D.* ii. 1.
6	F	**DUKE OF EDINBURGH** *b.* 1844. *" Is this the Captain in the Duke?"* . .	*All's W.* iv. 3.
7	S	**MRS. GLADSTONE'S CONVALESCENT HOSPITAL** ESTABLISHED, 1866. *"'Tis not enough to help the feeble up,* *But to support him after"* . .	*T. of A.* i. 1.
8	☲	**Eleventh Sunday after Trinity.** *" He that doth the ravens feed,* *Yea, providently caters for the sparrow,* *Be comfort to my age"* . . .	*A.Y.L.I.* ii. 3.
9	M	**ISAAK WALTON** *b.* 1593. *" Give me my angle"*	*A. & C.* ii. 5.
10	T	**SIR CHARLES JAMES NAPIER** *b.* 1782. *" He did look far into the service of the time,* *and was disciplined of the bravest"* .	*All's W.* i. 2.
11	W	**ELIHU BURRITT** *b.* 1811. *"'Tis no sin for a man to labour in his vocation"*	*Hen. IV.* i. 2.
12	Th	**GEORGE STEPHENSON** *d.* 1848. *" A rare engineer"*	*T. & C.* ii. 3.
13	F	**REV. ROWLAND HILL** *b.* 1744. *" Pleasant, pithy, and effectual"* . .	*T. the S.* iii. 1.
14	S	**LORD CLYDE** *d.* 1863. *" I will use the olive with the sword"* .	*T. of A.* v. 5.
15	☲	**Twelfth Sunday after Trinity.** *" God knows of pure devotion"*	2 *H. VI.* ii. 1.
16	M	**NAPOLEON I.** *b.* 1769. *" Thou wast born to conquer"* . .	*T. of A.* iv. 3.

AUGUST.

				A. SC.
17	T	THE PRINCES SMOTHERED IN THE TOWER, 1483. "*Foul and most* *Unnatural murder*"		*Ham.* i. 5.
18	W	EARL RUSSELL *b.* 1792. "*I have done the State some service*" . .		*Oth.* v. 2.
19	Th	SIR WALTER RALEIGH SET OUT ON HIS LAST VOYAGE, 1617. "*Daring, bold, and venturous*" . . .		*Ric. III.* iv. 4
20	F	ROBERT HERRICK *b.* 1591. "*The lines are very quaintly writ*" . . .		*2 G. of V.* ii. 1.
21	S	WILLIAM GIFFORD *b.* 1765. "*For I am nothing if not critical*" . . .		*Oth.* ii. 1.
22	☱	Thirteenth Sunday after Trinity. " *Devils soonest tempt, resembling* *Spirits of light*"		*L. L. L.* iv. 3.
23	M	DUKE OF BUCKINGHAM ASSASSINATED BY FEL- TON, 1628. "*No reckoning made, but sent to my account* *With all my imperfections on my head*" . .		*Ham.* i. 5.
24	T	WILBERFORCE *b.* 1759. "*Live all free men*"		*Jul. C.* iii. 1.
25	W	FARADAY *d.* 1867. "*That we find out the cause of this effect*" .		*Ham.* ii. 2.
26	Th	PRINCE CONSORT *b.* 1819. "*Wherever the bright sun of Heaven shall shine,* *His honour and the greatness of his name* *Shall be*"		*H. VIII.* v. 4.
27	F	OLIVER GOLDSMITH *b.* 1731. "*So let him rest, his faults lie gently on him*" .		*H. VIII.* iv. 2
28	S	LEIGH HUNT *d.* 1859. "*Child of fancy*"		*L. L. L.* i. 1.
29	☱	Fourteenth Sunday after Trinity. " *My comfort is, that Heaven will take our souls*"		*Ric. II.* iii. 1.
30	M	O. WENDELL HOLMES *b.* 1809. "*To my house to breakfast*" . . .		*M. Wiv.* iii. 3.
31	T	JOHN BUNYAN *d.* 1688. "*How like a dream is this I see*" . .		*2 G. of V.* v. 4.

SEPTEMBER.

1	W	**PARTRIDGE SHOOTING BEGINS.**	A. SC.
		" At the gun's report	
		Sever themselves, and madly sweep the sky" .	*M.N.D.* iii. 2.
2	Th	**GEN. HAYNAU AT BARCLAY'S BREWERY, 1850.**	
		" Thou wear a lion's hide! doff it, for shame,	
		And hang a calf's skin on those recreant limbs"	*K. John* iii. 1.
3	F	**OLIVER CROMWELL** *d.* 1658.	
		" A soldier firm and sound of heart" . .	*Hen. V.* iii. 6.
		" Speaking in deeds"	*T. & C.* iv. 5.
4	S	**HON. CHARLES TOWNSHEND** *d.* 1767.	
		" We,	
		Almost with ravish'd list'ning, could not find	
		His hour of speech a minute" . . .	*H. VIII.* i. 2.
5	☙	𝔉𝔦𝔣𝔱𝔢𝔢𝔫𝔱𝔥 𝔖𝔲𝔫𝔡𝔞𝔶 𝔞𝔣𝔱𝔢𝔯 𝔗𝔯𝔦𝔫𝔦𝔱𝔶.	
		" The Lord have mercy on me"	*Oth.* v. 2.
6	M	**ABDICATION OF FRANCIS II., 1860.**	
		" Outcast of Naples"	2 *H. VI.* v. 1.
7	T	**QUEEN ELIZABETH** *b.* 1533.	
		" She'll not be hit	
		With Cupid's arrow"	*R. & J.* i. 1.
8	W	**LINDLEY MURRAY** *b.* 1745.	
		" Show me now, William, some declensions of	
		your pronouns"	*M. W.* iv. 1.
9	Th	**BLOOMER COSTUME FIRST PUBLICLY WORN, 1849.**	
		" What fashion, Madam, shall I make your . . ?"	2 *G. of V.* ii. 7.
10	F	**MUNGO PARK** *b.* 1771.	
		" A man of travel"	*L. L. L.* v. 1.
11	S	**SIEGE OF DELHI, 1863.**	
		" Our cannon shall be bent	
		Against the brows of this resisting town" .	*K. John* ii. 1.
12	☙	𝔖𝔦𝔵𝔱𝔢𝔢𝔫𝔱𝔥 𝔖𝔲𝔫𝔡𝔞𝔶 𝔞𝔣𝔱𝔢𝔯 𝔗𝔯𝔦𝔫𝔦𝔱𝔶.	
		" Heaven, lay not my transgressions to his	
		charge" .	*K. John* i. 1.
13	M	**DANTE** *d.* 1321.	
		" Italy contains none so accomplished" .	*Cym.* i. 5.
14	T	**WELLINGTON** *d.* 1852.	
		" Whose life was England's glory" . .	1 *H. VI.* iv. 7.
15	W	**J. K. BRUNEL** *d.* 1859.	
		" Let him show	
		His skill in the construction" .	*Cym.* v. 5.

SEPTEMBER.

16	Th	**REVOLUTION IN SPAIN (1868), ISABELLA ESCAPES TO FRANCE.**	
		"And now the end of all, is bought thus dear	
		* * * * * . *	A. S?.
		By flight, I'll shun the danger which I fear".	*Per.* i. 1.
17	F	**DAILY TELEGRAPH REDUCED TO ONE PENNY; 1855.**	
		"Read o'er these articles" . . .	*Ric. II.* iv. 1.
18	S	**DR. JOHNSON** *b.* 1709.	
		"I am Sir Oracle,	
		And when I ope my lips let no dog bark!" .	*M. of V.* i. 1.
19	☽	**Seventeenth Sunday after Trinity.**	
		"God give you joy" . .	*Per.* ii. 5.
20	M	**LORD BROUGHAM** *b.* 1778.	
		"Appears sometimes like a lord; sometimes like	
		a lawyer; sometimes like a philosopher".	*T. of A.* ii. 2.
21	T	**SIR WALTER SCOTT** *d.* 1832.	
		"O, that he were here to write" . . .	*M. Ado* iv. 2.
22	W	**LORD CHESTERFIELD** *b.* 1694.	
		"Behaviour, what wert thou	
		Till this man showed thee" . . .	*L. L. L.* v. 2.
23	Th	**MALIBRAN** *d.* 1836.	
		"With all my heart I'll sit, and hear her sing"	*1 H. IV.* iii. 1.
24	F	**PROSECUTION OF MADAME RACHEL (1868) BY MRS. BORRODAILE.**	
		"Nay, never paint me now:	
		Where fair is not, praise cannot mend the brow"	*L. L. L.* iv. 1.
25	S	**GREAT EXHIBITION COMMENCED, 1850.**	
		"We have the Exhibition to examine" . .	*M. Ado* iv. 2.
26	☽	**Eighteenth Sunday after Trinity.**	
		"Men must endure	
		Their going hence, even as their coming hither"	*K. Lear* v. 2.
27.	M	**DR. VALPY** *b.* 1754.	
		"Cunning in Greek, Latin, and other languages"	*T. of S.* ii. 1.
28	T	**NEW RIVER COMPLETED, 1613.**	
		"Our best water, brought by conduits hither" .	*Corio.* ii. 3.
29	W	**MICHAELMAS DAY.**	
		"I smell some goose in this"	*L. L. L.* iii. 1.
30	Th	**AUGUSTE COMTE** *d.* 1857.	
		"There are more things in Heaven and earth, Horatio,	
		Than are dreamt of in your philosophy" .	*Ham.* i. 5.

OCTOBER.

1	F	MAJOR ANDRÉ EXECUTED, 1780.
		"*I do think that you might pardon him,*
		And neither Heaven nor man grieve at the mercy"

A. SC.
M. for M. ii. 2.

2	S	DR. CHANNING *d.* 1842.
		"*A noble spirit*" . . . . .

T. of A. i. 2.

3	S	Nineteenth Sunday after Trinity.
		"*Rest your minds in peace*" .

1 *H. VI.* i. 1.

4	M	GUIZOT *b.* 1787.
		"*There is a history in all men's lives*" . .

2 *H. IV.* iii. 1.

5	T	HORACE WALPOLE *b.* 1717.
		"*The visage of the times*" . . .

2 *H. IV.* ii. 3.

6	W	LOUIS PHILIPPE *b.* 1773.
		"*The world is full of rubs*
		My fortune runs against the bias" . .

Rich. II. iii. 4.

7	Th	EDGAR POE *d.* 1849.
		"*Wrapped in dismal thinkings*" . .

All's Well v. 3.

8	F	FIFTEEN ENGLISH MEN-OF-WAR FOUNDERED IN THE WEST INDIES, 1780.
		"'*Tis a vile thing to die, my gracious lord,*
		When men are unprepared and look not for it"

Ric. III. iii 2.

9	S	EDDYSTONE LIGHTHOUSE COMMENCED, 1759.
		"*Thou art a perpetual triumph! an everlasting*
		bonfire light" . . . .

1 *H. IV.* iii. 3.

10	S	Twentieth Sunday after Trinity.
		"*Love thyself last*" .

H. VIII. iii. 2.

11	M	SEA-SERPENT SEEN FROM H.M.S. "DÆDALUS," 1848.
		"*Were I in England now, and had but this fish*
		painted, not a holiday-fool there but would
		give a piece of silver" . . .

Tempest ii. 2.

12	T	ELIZABETH FRY *d.* 1841.
		"*I come to visit the afflicted spirits*
		Here in the prison: * * *that I may mini-*
		ster to them" . . . .

M. for M. ii. 3.

13	W	CANOVA *d.* 1822.
		"*Would you not deem it breathed? and that*
		those veins
		Did verily bear blood?" . . .

Win. T. v. 3.

14	Th	PENN *b.* 1644.
		"*Good dawning to thee, Friend!*" . .

K. Lear ii. 2.

15	F	BISHOPS RIDLEY AND LATIMER BURNT, 1555.
		"*We must be burnt for you*" . .

Corio. v. 1.

16	S	KOSCIUSKO *d.* 1817.
		"*A foe to tyrants, and my country's friend*" .

Jul. C. v. 4.

OCTOBER.

17	S	Twenty-first Sunday after Trinity.		A. SC.
		"*Kindness, nobler ever than revenge*"	•	*A. Y. L. I.* iv. 3.
18	M	PALMERSTON *d.* 1865.		
		"*He hath deserved worthily of his country*"	.	*Corio.* ii. 2.
19	T	GRACE DARLING *d.* 1842.		
		"*Her valiant courage, and undaunted spirit*		
		More than in woman commonly is seen"	.	1 *H. VI.* v. 5.
20	W	THOMAS HUGHES *b.* 1823.		
		"*He was quick mettle when he went to school*"	.	*Jul. C.* i. 2.
21	Th	BATTLE OF TRAFALGAR: NELSON KILLED, 1805.		
		"*Either a victory or else a grave*"	. . .	3 *H. IV.* ii. 2.
22	F	WALLER *d.* 1687.		
		"*Versing love to amorous Phillida*"	. .	*M. N. D.* ii. 2.
23	S	ROYAL EXCHANGE FOUNDED, 1667.		
		"*Where merchants most do congregate*"	. .	*M. of V.* i. 3.
24	S	Twenty-second Sunday after Trinity.		
		"*Great God, how just art Thou!*" .	.	2 *H. VI.* v. 1.
25	M	SIR JAMES GRAHAM *d.* 1861.		
		"*Letters should not be known*"	. . •	*Tempest* ii. 1.
		"*This day is called the Feast of* CRISPIAN"	. •	*Hen. V.* iv. 3.
26	T	HOGARTH *b.* 1764.		
		"*Whose end was to hold, as 'twere, the mirror up*		
		to nature; to show virtue her own feature,		
		scorn her own image, and the very age and		
		body of the time his form and pressure"	.	*Ham.* iii. 2.
27	W	J. T. DELANE *b.* 1817.		
		"*Order gave all things view*" .	. .	*H. VIII.* i. 1.
28	Th	JOHN LEECH *d.* 1864.		
		"*So excellent in art*"	. . . .	*H. VIII.* iv. 2.
29	F	JAMES BOSWELL *b.* 1740.		
		"*The babbling gossip*" .	. . .	*Twel. N.* i. 5.
30	S	EARL OF DUNDONALD *d.* 1860.		
		"*By Heaven you do me wrong*		
		* * * *		
		You charge me most unjustly"	. .	*Oth.* iv. 2.
31	S	Twenty-third Sunday after Trinity.		
		"*Forbear to judge, for we are sinners all*"	,	2 *H. VI.* iii. 3.

NOVEMBER.

1	M	GREAT EARTHQUAKE AT LISBON, 1763.	
		" The frame and huge foundation of the earth	A. SC.
		Shaked like a coward"	1 *H. IV.* iii. 1.
2	T	DR. HOOKER *d.* 1600.	
		" Famously enriched	
		With politic grave counsel" . .	*Ric. III.* ii. 3.
3	W	"SATURDAY REVIEW" FOUNDED, 1855.	
		" Lord Angelo is severe" . . .	*M. for M.* ii. 1.
4	Th	MENDELSSOHN *d.* 1847.	
		" That strain again; it had a dying fall;	
		O, it came o'er my ear like the sweet south	
		That breathes upon a bank of violets,	
		Stealing and giving odour" . . .	*Tw:l. N.* i. 1.
5	F	GUY FAWKES CONSPIRACY, 1605.	
		" The King hath note of all that they intend,	
		By interception, which they dream not of" .	*Hen. V.* ii. 2.
6	S	PRINCESS CHARLOTTE *d.* 1817.	
		" Alas! poor Princess"	*Cym.* ii. 1.
7	☰	Twenty-fourth Sunday after Trinity.	
		" Good angels guard thee"	*Ric. III.* v. 3.
8	M	MADAME ROLAND GUILLOTINED, 1793.	
		" Put me into everlasting liberty" . .	*M. Wiv.* iii. 3.
9	T	PRINCE OF WALES *b.* 1841.	
		" May he live	
		Longer than I have time to tell his years " .	*H. VIII.* ii. 1.
		LORD MAYOR'S DAY.	
		" The mayor towards Guildhall hies * * *	
		His banquet is prepared" . . .	*Ric. III.* iii. 5.
10	W	DR. CUMMING *b.* 1810.	
		" Let the vile world end,	
		And the premiséd flames of the last day	
		Knit earth and heaven together" . .	2 *H. VI.* v. 2.
11	Th	EARL OF BRIDGEWATER *b.* 1758.	
		" The full assurance of your faith " . .	*Tw:l. N.* iv. 3.
12	F	RICHARD BAXTER *b.* 1615.	
		" I know him for a man divine and holy " .	*M. for M.* v. 1.
13	S	WILLIAM ETTY *d.* 1849.	
		" His Art with Nature's workmanship at strife"	*Venus & Adon.*
14	☰	Twenty-fifth Sunday after Trinity.	
		" Seek the light of truth " .	*L. L. L.* i. 1.
15	M	WM. PITT, THE GREAT EARL OF CHATHAM, *b.* 1708.	
		" A bold spirit in a loyal breast " . .	*Rich. II.* i. 1.

NOVEMBER.

				A. SC.
16	T	JOHN BRIGHT *b.* 1811. *"He cannot flatter, he! An honest mind and plain,—he must speak truth"*	*K. Lear*	ii. 2.
17	W	SIR JOHN DE MANDEVILLE *d.* 1372. *"I can tell you strange news that you dreamed not of"*	*M. Ado.*	i. 2.
18	Th	SIR DAVID WILKIE *d.* 1785. *"A thousand moral paintings"*	*T. of A.*	i. 1.
19	F	SIR ALEXANDER COCKBURN APPOINTED LORD CHIEF JUSTICE, 1859. *"It doth appear you are a worthy judge"* .	*M. of V.*	iv. 1.
20	S	CHATTERTON *b.* 1752. *"Blasting in the bud, Losing his verdure even in the prime, And all the fair effects of future hopes"* . .	*2 G. of V.*	i. 1.
21	S	Twenty-sixth Sunday after Trinity. *"God shall be my hope, My stay, my guide, my lantern to my feet"* .	*2 H. VI.*	ii. 3.
22	M	SIR HENRY HAVELOCK *d.* 1857. *"O Thou! whose captain I account myself, Look on my forces with a gracious eye"* . .	*Ric. III.*	v. 3.
23	T	LAURENCE STERNE *d.* 1713. *"I can easier teach twenty what were good to be done, Than be one of the twenty to follow my own teaching"*	*M. of V.*	i. 2.
24	W	JOHN KNOX *d.* 1572. *"Away, away, Corruptors of my faith"*	*Cym.*	iii. 4.
25	Th	EDWARD ALLEYN, FOUNDER OF DULWICH COLLEGE, *d.* 1626. *"'Twere good you do so much for charity"* .	*M. of V.*	iv. 1.
26	F	JOHN ELWES *d* 1789. *"Decrepit miser! base, ignoble wretch!"* . .	*1 H. VI.*	v. 4.
27	S	BENEDICT *b.* 1804. *"I thank you for your music"* . .	*2 G. of V.*	iv. 2.
28	S	Advent Sunday. *"God is to be worshipped"*	*M. Ado.*	iii. 5.
29	M	LORD CHANCELLOR WOOD *b.* 1801. *"Equally indeed to all estates"* . .	*Ric. III.*	iii. 7.
30	T	MARK LEMON *b.* 1809. *"I am not only witty in myself, but the cause that wit is in other men"*	*2 H. IV.*	i. 2.

DECEMBER.

| 1 | W | PRINCESS OF WALES *b.* 1844. | A. SC. |
| | | "*Kind and dear Princess*" . . . . | *K. Lear* iv. 7. |

2 Th THE GLADSTONE MINISTRY FORMED, 1868.
"*Now join your hands, and with your hands
your hearts,
That no dissension hinder government*" . . 3 *H. VI.* iv. 6.

3 F THOMAS CARLYLE *b.* 1795.
"*A mint of phrases in his brain
    *   *   *   *   *
A man of fire-new words*" . . . . *L. L. L.* i. 1.

4 S MACKONOCHIE CASE COMMENCED, 1867.
"*Is your priesthood grown peremptory?
Churchmen so hot!*" . . . . . 2 *H. VI.* ii. 1.

5 ⸸ Second Sunday in Advent.
"*The time of life is short*" . . . 1 *H. IV.* v. 2.

6 M GENERAL PRIM *b.* 1814.
"*A most gallant leader*" . . . . 2 *H. IV.* iii. 2.

7 T MARSHAL NEY SHOT, 1815.
"*Noble, wise, valiant, and honest*" . . . *Jul. C.* iii. 1.

8 W FATHER MATTHEW *d.* 1856.
"*Here's that which is too weak to be a sinner,
Honest water! which ne'er left man i' the mire*" *T. of A.* i. 2.

9 Th MILTON *b.* 1608.
"*As imagination bodies forth
The forms of things unknown, the poet's pen
Turns them to shapes, and gives to airy nothing
A local habitation and a name*" . . . *M. N. D.* v. 1.

10 F CLARENDON *d.* 1674.
"*I am a man whom fortune hath cruelly
scratched*" . . . . . . *All's Well* v. 2.

11 S THE GREAT CONDÉ *d.* 1686.
"*Flower of warriors*" . . . . . *Corio.* i. 6.

12 ⸸ Third Sunday in Advent.
"*And death once dead, there's no more dying then*" *Poems.*

13 M DEAN STANLEY *b.* 1815.
"*A noble temper dost thou show*" . . . *K. John* v. 2.

14 T DEATH OF THE PRINCE CONSORT AT WINDSOR
CASTLE, 1861.
"*There's a great spirit gone*" . . . *A. & C.* i. 2.

15 W LORD COBHAM BURNT AS A LOLLARD, 1417.
"*Thou fall'st a blessed martyr*" . . . *H. VIII.* iii. 2.

DECEMBER.

			A. SC.
16	Th	GEORGE WHITFIELD *b.* 1714.	
		"*Devotion and right Christian zeal*" .	*Ric. III.* iii. 7.
17	F	FRANK BUCKLAND *b.* 1826.	
		"*Toads, bats, and beetles light upon you*"	*Tempest* i. 2.
18	S	PRINCE RUPERT *b.* 1619.	
		"*Rash, inconsiderate, fiery*" . . .	*K. John* ii. 1.
19	S	𝔉ourth 𝔖unday in 𝔄dvent.	
		"*God be with you all*" .	*Hen. V.* iv. 3.
20	M	NAPOLEON III. ELECTED PRESIDENT. 1848.	
		"*Some are born great, some achieve greatness, and some have greatness thrust upon them*" .	*Twel. N.* ii. 5.
21	T	EARL BEACONSFIELD *b.* 1805.	
		"*What he is, indeed, More suits you to conceive, than me to speak of*"	*A.Y.L.I.* i. 2.
22	W	DR. TAIT *b.* 1811, INSTALLED ARCHBISHOP OF CANTERBURY, FEB., 1869.	
		"*He is worthy of it*"	*H. VIII.* v. 2.
23	Th	ROBERT BARCLAY *b.* 1648.	
		"*The love I have in doing good*" .	*M. for M.* iii. 1.
24	F	CAPTURE OF MADEIRA, 1807.	
		"*The climate's delicate; the air most sweet: Fertile the isle*"	*Win. T.* iii. 1.
25	S	CHRISTMAS DAY.	
		"*That season comes Wherein our Saviour's birth is celebrated*" .	*Hamlet* i. 1.
26	S	𝔉irst 𝔖unday after 𝔠hristmas.	
		"*Heaven has an end in all*" . .	*H.VIII.* ii. 1.
27	M	CHARLES LAMB *d.* 1834.	
		"*A fellow of infinite jest,—of most excellent fancy*"	*Hamlet* v. 1.
28	T	LORD MACAULAY *d.* 1859.	
		"*Turn him to any cause of policy, The Gordian knot of it he will unloose Familiar as his garter*" . . .	*Hen. V.* i. 1.
29	W	GLADSTONE *b.* 1809.	
		"*The good I stand on is my truth and honesty*" .	*H. VIII.* v. 1.
30	Th	WICKLIFFE *d.* 1384.	
		"*Gave his pure soul unto his captain, Christ, Under whose colours he had fought so long*" .	*Ric. II.* iv. 1.
31	F	"*Here is my journey's end*" . .	*Othello* v. 2.

www.ingramcontent.com/pod-product-compliance
Lightning Source LLC
Chambersburg PA
CBHW021451090426
42739CB00009B/1719